The Abduction

Le Rapt

First published in 2020
by Southword Editions
The Munster Literature Centre
Frank O'Connor House, 84 Douglas Street
Cork, Ireland

Original texts by Maram al-Masri
Translated from the Syrian Arabic by the author
Published by
Éditions Bruno Doucey
Cours d'Alsace-Lorraine,
67 rue de Reuilly,
Paris 75012
Copyright © Éditions Bruno Doucey, 2015
The texts in Arabic and the translations in French

Copyright © Theo Dorgan, 2018
The English translation

Copyright © John Minihan, 2017
Author photograph

Set in Adobe Caslon 12pt

ISBN 978-1-905002-79-5

The Abduction

Translation by Theo Dorgan

of

Le Rapt

by Maram al-Masri

SOUTHWORDeditions

Contents

Foreword	*6*
1	*11*
2	*12*
3	*13*
4	*14*
5	*15*
6	*16*
7	*17*
8	*18*
9	*19*
10	*20*
11	*21*
12	*22*
13	*23*
14	*24*
15	*25*
16	*26*
17	*27*
18	*28*
19	*29*
20	*30*
21	*31*
22	*32*
23	*33*
24	*34*
25	*35*
26	*36*
27	*38*
28	*39*
29	*40*
30	*41*

31	*42*
32	*43*
33	*44*
34	*45*
35	*46*
36	*47*
37	*48*
38	*49*
39	*50*
40	*51*
The Bread of Letters	*52*

Foreword

This is Maram al-Masri's ninth collection, deeply personal as all her work is, drawn from her own life. Autobiography, then, yet more often than not, her touch is so light, the poems read as if written by a ghost passing through the language and through the world. Her subjects here are grief and love, the truths and impossibility of each and both. More particularly, the grief of a loving mother cruelly separated from her infant son, her love for her absent son, the need to find a language of love that may pass between them when he is restored to her embrace.

When the young mother sought a separation from her husband, he abducted their infant son and went back with the child to his native Syria. Years later, the child returns. In the intervening years his mother must live in the shadows of daily grief, the sunlight of carefully-hoarded memories—and then, when the child returns, she must make the difficult connection between the child she has kept alive in memory and the boy as he actually is when, eventually, he is restored to her.

al-Masri, here as elsewhere, writes with extreme simplicity and economy of means — a modest vocabulary, a tone that registers extremes of grief and joy in a voice that seems only rarely to rise above a whisper.

Grief is a kind of exile, and these are the poems of an exile, of a woman driven by cruelty into a world where her rights as a mother are negated—the right to give love, the right to receive love, the right to determine her life in accord with her own independent sense of what is proper and just.

And yet, in and through the poems, she is somehow vindicated and saved.

As to the text: al-Masri usually makes her poems, simultaneously, in both Arabic and French. I have translated from the French, having no Arabic. As the second section of the original *Le Rapt* is in the French of Najeh Jegam, with the participation of al-Masri and Bruno Doucey, I have chosen to translate only the first and third sections. In this way, my engagement is only with the poems of the original author.

Her French only rarely employs standard punctuation, which works in the original but by its strangeness would draw excessive attention to itself were I to follow her in English. I have stuck to standard punctuation in the translations, by and large, but in individual instances I have left the poems unpunctuated as they are in the original, so that the English reader may get a feel for the effect produced in the French versions. In occasional instances, very few, I have altered the lineation in the interests of clarity. My aim at all times has been to convey not only the sense of the originals but the tone, linguistic and emotional, of these extraordinary poems.

—Theo Dorgan
Ikaria, 2018

*Your children are not yours. They are the children of life.
And life does not live in the house of yesterday.*

1

Nine months,

and life is taking root in the guts
as a poem grows in the imagination.
Nine months, and a body is growing inside another body.
Nine months, and the waiting is knitting hope to dream.

Nine months for silence to grow
almost to the cry
like a loaf of bread rising
like a moon round and full
coming to term.
Nine months
for a heart to pulse
inside a heart.
Nine months
for a life to begin.

2

We sow
she sprouts
she grows
she explodes
she gives birth
to an infant in a poem.

Between her thighs
it flows
like a waterfall,
a small body
naked,
hot.
He cries
"I am here".

3

He has begun to speak to me
with his eight small teeth,
drool on his lips.
He tells me with his eyes
things that seem to him important,
perhaps he is speaking to me of war
and the children born
to die every day,
or perhaps he is telling me
of islands far away,
of birds
of dreams
of crises
of famines.

I do not know if he wants to tell me
that the future will be sunny,
that a day will come
when people will live in peace.

He is occupied
with making his ten fingers move,
with convincing me that love is the natural fruit
of the tree of life,
and that he is happy
to have come to this world.

Then, suddenly, he has me entangled,
burrowing his head into my chest,
begging me to take him in my arms.
In that instant I understand
all that he wishes to say to me.

4

I hugged him
I felt his calm respiration
dampen my neck

I squeezed him to my breast
I passed my hand over his face
I touched with my fingers
the innocence of his skin,
an instant of eternity flowered
in a desert day.

I have always his hands
on my shoulders,
and on my chin
the pain from his little teeth.

5

Duckling

you waddle,
you hang on to my finger,
if I let go, you fall.
I pick you up and I hum
you walk, hesitant,
like a duck.
You fall and you pick yourself up,
we try again
fall, get up again.

It is like this,
life,
my little urchin;
before we can become
horses, galloping.

6

When I catch him in the act,
occupied with disorganising
the contents of drawers
and throwing everywhere all that his hands
can reach,
he runs away
hiding his face, then turning gently
to observe our reaction.
When he sees a smile on our lips
he returns, his arms extended, imploring us,
invoking our weakness—
before he climbs up on us
as if nothing has happened.

7

Come on, sun,
wake up!
Let your yellow hair float out
over the frozen shoulders of earth,
over the houses and the streets.
Heat up again the stones, the asphalt—
dance, sun, blaze!
Make this day a good day,
because far from this cold wall,
in a field of colours
where the sky is made of tales
and where the trees are poems,
I mean to take my child for a walk.

8

In such beautiful weather
I need my small child
so that I can rejoice with him
in the sky, the water,
the people.

In weather sad as this
I need my small child
so that I can rejoice,
and make him rejoice,
in life.

9

Dance, dance
my son,
you were born
to learn from the birds
how to fly.

Dance, dance
my son,
so that the troubled heart of the world
may calm itself
to the rhythm
of your steps.

Dance, dance
my son,
you must learn how to fly.

10

I talk to him
as to a friend,
I converse with him
as one speaks to a grown up.
I ask him if he likes my red dress,
its length,
if it would be better longer?
After I've put on my make up, I ask him
how he finds me,
if I am beautiful?
Primping his belly
and his cheeks
with my red lips
makes me joyous.
All this time, he is occupied with taking
the spoons out of the drawer.

11

With these two hands
I have prepared your suitcase for you,
your father has told me
he's taking you on a short trip
to a city by the sea.

Into your case I have put
your best clothes
because my little one is going for a walk by the sea.

I have also put in
the cakes that you love
and everything you might need
because my little one is going for a walk by the sea.

With these two hands
I have placed you in your stroller
happy
because my little one is going for a walk by the sea.

The evening passed—
and until this day
my little one's stroller has not come back.

12

O human brothers!
O world!
I had a child
I hid him in my belly
he shared my body
I nourished him with my blood.
I had him share in my dreams
I sang for him, he smiled
I carried him, he stopped crying.

He was torn from my arms,
I ceased to sing.

13

There is war in Rwanda
and me, I am dining.
There is war in Yugoslavia
and me, I am smiling.
There is war in Palestine
and me, I am asleep.

Since you were taken
the war is in me.

14

In the evening
when my flowers have faded
I curl up under a heavy cover,
I close my eyes,
I ask myself:
what dreams
can possibly bring me
sleep?

15

Promise me
if I close my eyes
that you will run into my arms
to light up
this dark world.

Promise me
if I open my eyes
you will stay.

16

I sent you
my love
in the post,
I had exchanged it for small toys
so that you could play,
I had exchanged it for a woolen polo-neck
so that you would be warm.

I sent you my love
in the post,
I had exchanged it for two boxes of aspirin
a toothbrush
cakes, chocolate,
a bicycle—
did you receive the package?

17

If I smile while you are far away
it means that a shadow
has passed in front of me,
you in your white wrappings
and the toy you drag behind you.

If I smile when you are far away
that is not to say that I have forgotten you;
sometimes
it is to say
that your presence
even at a distance of thousands of kilometres
can bring me happiness.

18

Forgive me, my little one,
if I haven't
come to you quickly,
on foot the way is long
and I don't have the wherewithal to buy tickets.

Forgive me, my little one,
that excuse
must seem feeble to you;
of course
I could come on foot
or borrow the money
or make some economies,
stop smoking
(even though I don't smoke)
or even sell my mother's jewels
to pay for the tickets.

Forgive them, my little one,
when I came
they would not let me see you.

19

Far from my arms
you sleep in a bed that is not yours,
you no longer see my face
nor my eyes that you would look into with such love.
You can no longer take my hand
as you used to do
before falling asleep.

At night you will wake
and murmur 'Mother',
to a woman who is not me.

Far from my eyes
you will grow
you will go to school
and I will not be waiting for you at the gate,
you will fall ill
and I will not be worrying there beside you.

I will recognise neither your face nor your voice
I will not recognise your smell
nor what you wear;
you will rest in my memory
the eighteen month old child
they kidnapped from me.

20

I came back to the house
after a night out with friends,
I had hurried back to check on you.

I opened the door gently
listening
to find in the silence
that you were sleeping deeply.

Tonight
I stepped into your room
the bed was calm
covered with your soul
—and somehow I swear
I could hear your breathing.

21

Every morning
I wake
wanting to prepare your breakfast

Every morning
I open my eyes
I want you to wet
my face with kisses

Every morning I wake up
and I want you to have already woken me.
For a long time now
I have chopped my sleep
into a thousand pieces.

22

You remember
that little boy
who lived with his parents next door to us?
When his mother would leave him with us
while she did her shopping,
I used to put you together
to play and babble.

You remember
how he was quiet and wise?
He would never complain,
nor get annoyed even when you took his toys
or when you would lean on him to stand up

He was called Salim,
his mother Josephine, a resigned woman.
Like me she had tasted bitterness.
When I learned that his father had kidnapped him
and sent him far away to his Grandmother's house
I wept for him.
I did not realise, in that moment,
that I was pouring out my first tears
for you.

23

Under the bed
I found your teddy bear
that you would embrace and cover with kisses
that you would talk to, your eyes wide open,
waiting for the angel of sleep to come.

You remember how he could
stop your storm of crying
when I would show him to you and shake him.
Ah how the night of your eyes gleamed,
and how the falls of Niagara
would cease falling.
You'd grab him from my hands
holding him close to you,
appeased.
He was your companion
to face down the night,
your silent friend
whom you would neglect
when you were preoccupied,
whom you would search out when sad.

The teddy bear and the angel of sleep,
you are searching for them always.

24

I am not that old,
so why
do I feel as if I am?
Why have the hairs in my dream turned white?
Why has the fire in my eyes
turned into cinders?

I am that old,
so why
do I no longer taste honey in my life?
Why is the song of morning
that I used to hum
changed into silence?

25

I do not wish to die,
I want my child to recognise me
the day he returns
and will see me.

I do not wish to die.
I will not do as my mother did,
I have a child
even though he is not in my arms
and one day
for certain
he will have need of me.

26

I promise you mother,
all is well.

Let your body repose as much as possible,
sleep gently
and do not let nightmares disturb your peace.

It isn't difficult, tonight,
to free your soul,
to let it tour the house

Your little children have grown up,
the eldest boy got married just after you left us,
you knew his wife, who was my friend.
Now they have two children,
he gave the first-born his father's name.

The second, whose absence made you weep with worry,
you can be proud of him
because he, too, is married.
You would not know his wife, but if you did
you would love her,
he has a child to whom he has given his father's name

As for the third, so spoiled,
it's true he doesn't work but don't worry yourself,
one day he will—
and don't be surprised if one day he marries,
perhaps he will give his father's name
to his first-born child.

I don't know if you know
that my sister and I
both also married.
Me, I'm divorced—
don't get into a panic,
it's not so bad
except that if you'd been there
they would not have taken my child.
It's not worth it, making yourself sad
where you are, you're far from pain and time.
I saw your friend last night,
my God how she's changed!
She has grown old and begun to lose her teeth,
but you, young woman,
you will always be as you were when you closed your eyes.
Perhaps you've done well,
like this you will not see, even if
I tell you otherwise,
that my father also has married
and that we are truly orphans without you.

27

I no longer have the patience
to do my housework
I not longer have the energy
to put out the rubbish
I no longer have the strength
to put up with jokes
that don't make me laugh
I can no longer give birth
to greetings that colour the day
nor have I a breast that gives milk.

So I swing my arms
and there is no child in my lap
I look at the window beyond
that I have not cleaned for a long time.
The world is cold.

28

From my window
I see houses
their windows are often closed
I imagine what moves
behind their thick walls
I see a man returning home
and a woman going out
wearing a black coat
they have two children,
life has permitted that they may watch them grow.

A house like mine
that perhaps conceals wounds
perhaps hides stories.

One Sunday
the day of celebrating love
I saw the man coming home
with a bouquet of flowers,
walking towards his house.

A house unlike mine,
dressed in joy.

29

I wait for you when I wake
I wait for you when I sleep
I wait for you when I smile
I wait for you when I weep
I wait for you

When I do not wait for you
I wait for you like a page in a book
like a hunger of long duration
I wait for you like a breast engorged with milk
I wait for you like a flood
I wait for you like a party dress
I wait for you like a letter unread
I wait for you like hope
I wait for you like a hot meal
I wait for you like a daybreak
I wait for you
like a mother

30

Evening no longer has your eyes,
resting between your eyelids.
Evening no longer has a home,
it saunters
in its black dress into my heart

The evening that sleeps upon my shoulder
resembles your hair.
I would like to bury myself there,
to inhale your smell,
to wake in the morning
damp with your kisses

My evening no longer holds a tree
in whose shadow I could play
since you are gone.

31

Blessed are they who sleep deeply—
me, I sleep like the babysitters of the world,
eyes half-closed,
like a mother stretched out
with a new-born in her arms, suckling at her breast,
her ears attentive to his breathing.

32

First encounter

How you have grown, my son,
you have grown for thirteen years
and now your mouth
is full of teeth
the clothes that I kept for you
no longer fit
nor do your shoes

Do you think
we would recognise one another
if we were to meet by chance?

33

Look at me,
I am she who brought you into the world
who gave you milk

Look at your brothers
I have spoken so much of them
say 'bonjour' to them in French
it will be enough
to kiss them
or to exchange smiles.

They do not resemble you
you are more brown
but if one looks carefully
one sees that you share
the same traits.

Let's go,
repeat their names after me:
Mathieu, yes Mathieu,
Guill … aume,
you see, it's not so difficult
to speak
the language of love

34

Five years after our encounter

I moved away from the noise
he followed me
he sat near me
I dared to put my head on his shoulder
I wanted to breathe his air
and retrieve the faint smell of his infancy

I took his hands in mine
they were moist and sticky
he started to count my fingers
to him I had thousands

Out of a silence disturbed
only by the chatter of his heart
and his breathing,
he asked in his trembling voice:
"are you afraid to love me?"

How could a woman like me
be afraid to love
in whom are found living
all paths
all songs
all kisses
all smiles?
I answered, "yes".

He nodded his head,
smiling,
so that all the words came tumbling around us
like feathers from a wounded bird.

Then he said,
"me, too."

35

To confront so much pain,
to shatter the statue of sorrow,
I sprinkle my smile
like flower pollen
on the tops of trees
electricity pylons
pavements,
over faces of passers-by
bread
my cup of coffee.

To be worthy of love,
I offer love.

36

Every morning
I cover myself in a dew of tears
every day I weep
in the streets
in the Metro
at the cinema
in bed
in dreams
in tenderness
but
I distribute my smiles
like a postman.

Every day I suicide a little,
to stay alive

37

At my door two suitcases
and a young man
tall and thin
dark brown
hesitant, like someone who has lost his way.

At my door, two worn suitcases
like the clothes of a dockworker
in the port of a poor city.

They smell of far-off places
memories
histories,
like a prisoner's chains.

A young dark brown man
with black hair
his black eyes swimming
in a white sea,

he knocks on the door
of my heart

38

The world is hard, my son,
hard as the magazine of a machine gun,
hard as the walls of a detention centre,
hard as a look of contempt;
I did not ask you to be patient until you could join me
I did not tell you little plants
are easily crushed
I did not tell you to come when you were strong.
Here we love those with diplomas
we love those with bank accounts—
I tell you the drowned
cannot save
the drowned.

Immigrant,
you will always be
looked upon with suspicion,
I did not tell you that immigrants arrive
fragile as infants.

39

To love
is to give to an other
the possibility of doing without you.
To love, it is to prepare yourself
for abandonment.

40

Why do we love them?

We love them because we have seen them
as small cotton bundles in our hands
we look at them, sometimes, as rare objects
and other times we look at them
and wish they might become other,
like cinema actors
like photocopies of our dreams.
Nevertheless, we love them.

We love them even if they grow ugly
if they grow obese
if they hide behind their beards
if they are sombre and violent as a slap.

We love them with their smelly shoes
with their acne
with their illnesses
with their failures.

We love them, mentally handicapped,
we love them even when they are wrong
even when they take drugs,
when they lose themselves
and even when they
are lost.

The Bread of Letters

I

Who will tell the trees they are guilty
for having let fall their leaves,
who will accuse the sea of abandoning its shells on the sand?

I, mother-woman, woman-mother,
with two breasts for pleasure
two breasts for maternity
who gives the milk of music
tells stories
explains games
clarifies feelings
and the grammar of thoughts.
I, who am woman voluptuous tender,
virtuous and sinner,
with my mouth
I give to eat the bread of letters,
consonants and vowels,
phrases, synonyms and comparisons.

Who will accuse me,
I who make a gift of my body
to love?

II

The act of writing,
is it not a scandalous act in itself?

To write,
it is learning to know oneself in the most intimate thoughts

Yes I am scandalous
because I point to my truth and my nakedness as a woman,

yes I am scandalous
because I cry my sorrow and my hope
my desire, my hunger and my thirst.

To write
is to describe the multiple faces of man
the beautiful and the ugly
the tender and the cruel.

To write is to die in front of a person
upon whom you look, unmoved,

it is to drown in sight of a boat that passes close
without seeing you.

To write
is to be the boat that will save
the drowning.

To write
is to live on a cliff's edge
clinging to a blade
of grass.